E
Mae

MW01235660

Geese Find the Missing Piece

School Time Riddle Rhymes

by Marco and Giulio Maestro
pictures by Giulio Maestro

HarperTrophy®
An Imprint of HarperCollinsPublishers

HarperCollins®, ☂®, Harper Trophy®, and I Can Read Book®
are registered trademarks of HarperCollins Publishers Inc.

Geese Find the Missing Piece
School Time Riddle Rhymes
Text copyright © 1999 by Marco and Giulio Maestro
Illustrations copyright © 1999 by Giulio Maestro
Printed in the U.S.A. All rights reserved.

Library of Congress Cataloging-in-Publication Data
Maestro, Marco.
   Geese find the missing piece : school time riddle rhymes / by Marco and Giulio
Maestro ; pictures by Giulio Maestro.
      p.   cm. — (An I can read book)
   Summary: Rhyming riddles answer questions about a variety of animals at school.
   ISBN 0-06-026220-6. — ISBN 0-06-026221-4 (lib. bdg.) — ISBN 0-06-443707-8 (pbk.)
   1. Riddles, Juvenile.   2. Animals—Juvenile humor.   3. Schools—Juvenile humor.
[1. Animals—Wit and humor.   2. Schools—Wit and humor.   3. Riddles.   4. Jokes.]
I. Maestro, Giulio.   II. Title.   III. Series.
PN6371.5.M235   1999   98-41513
818'.5402—dc21   CIP
                                                                            AC

First Harper Trophy edition, 2000

Visit us on the World Wide Web!
www.harperchildrens.com

Geese Find the Missing Piece

School Time Riddle Rhymes

Where do polar bears
learn their ABCs?

At a **cool** . . .

school!

What does Polly say to Polly
when they meet at school?

We have the **same** . . .

name.

How do the noisy ducks
play with blocks?

They **stack** while they . . .

quack.

10

How does Bear make a big mess
at playtime?

He **knocks** down all the . . .

Crash!

blocks.

How is the puzzle finished?

The **geese** find the missing . . .

piece.

Where can you read lots of words?

Take a **look** in a . . .

book.

What does Penguin use to measure?

She uses a **cooler** . . .

ruler.

18

Why is Crocodile loud at snack time?

He **crunches** when he . . .

crunch

crunch

crunch

crunch

munches.

20

What color is strawberry punch?

The **drink** is . . .

pink.

What happens when Lion

spills the juice?

He gets a **stain** on his . . .

mane.

What is Gorilla's favorite flavor?

The **ape** loves . . .

grape.

How do Turtle and Rabbit

get ready for rest time?

Before their **naps**,

they take off their . . .

caps.

Where do kittens rest?

Little **cats** lie down on . . .

mats.

How does the teacher

make two kinds of music?

She **hums** as she . . .

hum

strum

strums.

How does the class

take a long walk?

They walk in single **file** for a . . .

mile.

What does Snake

like to do best at recess?

She loves to **glide** down the . . .

slide.

36

How does Lizard

take his friend for a ride?

He carries **Snail** on his . . .

tail.

Why does the teacher

take his class to the sea?

So he can **teach** at the . . .

beach.

Why does Ladybug

practice writing the alphabet?

So she can make each **letter** . . .

better.

Why is Panda's picture
hard to see?

She uses very **faint** . . .

paint.

How do Hippo and Heron
have fun in art?

They **play** with . . .

45

clay.

What does the driver

say on the way home?

School

"I'm glad there is no **fuss** on this . . .

Bus

bus!"

DATE DUE

JAN 4 '05			
JAN 18 '05			
FEB 24			
MAR 22 '05			
MAY 6 '05			
MAR 3 '06			
NOV 27 '07			

DEMCO 38-296